Dedication
To all those who ever struggled with learning a foreign language and to Wolfgang Karfunkel

Also by Yatir Nitzany

Conversational Spanish Quick and Easy

Conversational French Quick and Easy

Conversational Italian Quick and Easy

Conversational Portuguese Quick and Easy

Conversational German Quick and Easy

Conversational Dutch Quick and Easy

Conversational Norwegian Quick and Easy

Conversational Danish Quick and Easy

Conversational Russian Quick and Easy

Conversational Ukrainian Quick and Easy

Conversational Bulgarian Quick and Easy

Conversational Polish Quick and Easy

Conversational Hebrew Quick and Easy

Conversational Yiddish Quick and Easy

Conversational Armenian Quick and Easy

Conversational Arabic Quick and Easy

Conversational Spanish Quick and Easy
The Most Innovative Technique to Learn the Spanish Language

Part III

YATIR NITZANY

Translated by:
Semadar Mercedes Friedman

Interior Design:
Menachem Otto

Copyright © 2019
Yatir Nitzany
All rights reserved.
ISBN 13: 978-1951244484
Printed in the United States of America

Foreword

About Myself

For many years I struggled to learn Spanish, and I still knew no more than about twenty words. Consequently, I was extremely frustrated. One day I stumbled upon this method as I was playing around with word combinations. Suddenly, I came to the realization that every language has a certain core group of words that are most commonly used and, simply by learning them, one could gain the ability to engage in quick and easy conversational Spanish.

I discovered which words those were, and I narrowed them down to three hundred and fifty that, once memorized, one could connect and create one's own sentences. The variations were and are *infinite*! By using this incredibly simple technique, I could converse at a proficient level and speak Spanish. Within a week, I astonished my Spanish-speaking friends with my newfound ability. The next semester I registered at my university for a Spanish language course, and I applied the same principles I had learned in that class (grammar, additional vocabulary, future and past tense, etc.) to those three hundred and fifty words I already had memorized, and immediately I felt as if I had grown wings and learned how to fly.

At the end of the semester, we took a class trip to San José, Costa Rica. I was like a fish in water, while the rest of my classmates were floundering and still struggling to converse. Throughout the following months, I again applied the same principle to other languages—French, Portuguese, Italian, and Arabic, all of which I now speak proficiently, thanks to this very simple technique.

This method is by far the fastest way to master quick and easy conversational language skills. There is no other technique that compares to my concept. It is effective, it worked for me, and it will work for you. Be consistent with my program, and you too will succeed the way I and many, many others have.

Table of Contents

Introduction to the Program 9

Introduction to the Spanish Language 11

Memorization Made Easy 12

Spanish Pronunciation 13

The Program

- Office 15
- School 19
- Profession 21
- Business 25
- Sports 29
- Outdoor Activities 33
- Electrical Devices 35
- Tools 37
- Auto 41
- Nature 43
- Animals 45
- Religion, Holidays, and Traditions 49
- Wedding and Relationship 53
- Politics 49
- Military 53

Basic Grammatical Requirements of the Spanish Language 57

Conclusion 63

Note from the Author 64

Introduction to the Program

You have now reached Part 3 of Conversational Spanish Quick and Easy. In Part 1 you learned the 350 words that could be used in an infinite number of combinations. In Part 2 you moved on to putting these words into sentences. You learned how to ask for help when your house was hit by a hurricane and how to find the emergency services. For example, if you need to go to a hospital, you have now been provided with sentences and the vocabulary for talking to doctors and nurses and dealing with surgery and health issues. When you get to the hospital, you can tell the health services, "The hurricane caused a lot of destruction and damage in its path," and "We used the hurricane shelter for refuge."

In this third book in the series, you will find the culmination of this foreign language course that is based on a system using key phrases used in day-to-day life. You can now move on to further topics such as things you would say in an office. This theme is ideal if you've just moved to Spanish for a new job. You may be about to sit at your desk to do an important task assigned to you by your boss but you have forgotten the details you were given. Turn to your colleagues and say, "I have to write an important email but I forgot my password." Then, if the reply is "Our secretary isn't here today. Only the receptionist is here but she is in the bathroom," you'll know what is being said and you can wait for help. By the end of the first few weeks, you'll have at your disposal terminology that can help reflect your experiences. "I want to retire already," you may find yourself saying at coffee break on a Monday morning after having had to go to your bank manager and say, "I need a small loan in order to pay my mortgage this month."

I came up with the idea of this unique system of learning foreign languages as I was struggling with my own attempt to learn Spanish. When playing around with word combinations I discovered 350 words that when used together could make up an infinite number of sentences. From this beginning, I was able to start speaking in a new language. I then practiced and found that I could use the same technique with other languages, such as French, Portuguese, Italian and Arabic. It was a revelation.

This method is by far the easiest and quickest way to master other languages and begin practicing conversational language skills.

The range of topics and the core vocabulary are the main components of this flawless learning method. In Part 3 you have a chance to learn how to relate to people in many more ways. Sports, for example, are very important for keeping healthy and in good spirits. The social component of these types of activities should not be underestimated at all. You will, therefore, have much help when you meet some new people, perhaps in a bar, and want to say to them, "I like to watch basketball games," and "Today are the finals of the Olympic Games. Let's see who wins the World Cup."

For sports, the office, and for school, some parts of conversation are essential. What happens when you need to get to work but don't have any clean clothes to wear because of malfunctions with the machinery. What you need is to be able to pick up the phone and ask a professional or a friend, "My washing machine and dryer are broken so maybe I can wash my laundry at the public laundromat." When you finally head out after work for some drinks and meet a nice new man, you can say, "You can leave me a voicemail or send me a text message."

Hopefully, these examples help show you how reading all three parts of this series in combination will prepare you for all you need in order to boost your conversational learning skills and engage with others in your newly learned language. The first two books have been an important start. This third book adds additional vocabulary and will provide the comprehensive knowledge required.

The Spanish Language

Spanish originated in Spain, and it closely resembles Portuguese, as both are Latin in their derivation and, therefore, Romance languages. The Spanish language was spread during the 1500s by Spanish colonialists coming from Spain to South America. Since then, the language has grown and is now the fourth most-spoken language in the world. Spanish is still rising in popularity, as it has 98 million non-native speakers and 402 million native speakers. Don't you want to be a member of the ever-growing population of Spanish speakers? Now you can be, if you follow the simple instructions of this program.

Memorization Made Easy

There is no doubt the three hundred and fifty words in my program are the required essentials in order to engage in quick and easy basic conversation in any foreign language. However, some people may experience difficulty in the memorization. For this reason, I created Memorization Made Easy. This memorization technique will make this program so simple and fun that it's unbelievable! I have spread the words over the following twenty pages. Each page contains a vocabulary table of ten to fifteen words. Below every vocabulary box, sentences are composed from the words on the page that you have just studied. This aids greatly in memorization. Once you succeed in memorizing the first page, then proceed to the second page. Upon completion of the second page, go back to the first and review. Then proceed to the third page. After memorizing the third, go back to the first and second and repeat. And so on. As you continue, begin to combine words and create your own sentences in your head. Every time you proceed to the following page, you will notice words from the previous pages will be present in those simple sentences as well, because repetition is one of the most crucial aspects in learning any foreign language. Upon completion of your twenty pages, *congratulations,* you have absorbed the required words and gained a basic, quick-and-easy proficiency and you should now be able to create your own sentences and say anything you wish in the Spanish language. This is a crash course in conversational Spanish, and it works!

Reading and Pronunciation

The pronunciation of Spanish, in comparison to the English language, is more or less the same. There are, however, a few exceptions that are listed below. Please read and familiarize yourself with the rules of Spanish pronunciation.

CE is pronounced as "se." *Él dice* is pronounced as "él di-se."
G when followed by *e* or *i* sounds like the letter *h* in English, like "hot." For example, *general* is pronounced as "he-nere-ral."
H is silent. For example, *hacer* is pronounced as acer
J is pronounced similar to the *ch* in German and in Hebrew ("loch," "channuka," and "yacht"). For example, the English word "garden", translated *jardin* in Spanish, would sound like "chardin." The sound is a little difficult to pronounce for non-Spanish speakers. Tip: pronounce as if you are coughing up phlegm in the back of your throat. The English word "job", translated *trabajo*, is pronounced as "tra-ba-cho."
Ñ is pronounced as "ny." For example, "morning," *mañana*, sounds like "ma-ny-ana."
LL is pronounced as "ye." For example, "to arrive," *llegar*, sounds like "ye-gar." However, in some Spanish countries, they pronounce it as "je"; *llegar* would be pronounced as "je-gar."
RR is hard to pronounce for non-Spanish speakers, but an easy Tip is that the pronunciation is similar to the sound of a starting car engine, "rrrrrr." "Dog," *perro*, would be pronounced as "pe-rrrr-o."
V is pronounced as "b." *Victor* would be pronounced as "Biktor."
Z is pronounced as "s." For example "shoe" / *zapato*, would be pronounced as "sapato."

OFFICE - OFICINA

Boss - (male) Jefe **/ (female)** jefa
Employee - Empleado / (**female**) empleada
Staff - Personal
Meeting - Reunión / encuentro
Conference room - Sala de conferencias
Secretary - Secretario **/ (f)** secretaria **/ Receptionist -** Recepcionista
Schedule - Calendario
Calendar - Calendario
Supplies - Suministros
Pen - Bolígrafo / pluma / **Ink -** Tinta
Pencil - Lápiz / **Eraser -** Borrador
Desk - Escritorio **/ Cubicle -** Cubículo
Chair - Silla
Office furniture - Muebles de oficina
Business card - Tarjeta de visita
Lunch break - Pausa para almorzar
Days off - Días de descanso
Briefcase - Maletín
Bathroom - Cuarto de baño

My boss asked me to hand in the paperwork.
Mi jefe me pidió que entrege el papeleo.
Our secretary isn't here today. The receptionist is here but she is in the bathroom.
Nuestra secretaria no está aquí hoy. La recepcionista está aquí pero ella está en el baño.
The employee meeting can take place in the conference room.
La reunión de empleados puede tener lugar en la sala de conferencias.
My business cards are inside my briefcase.
Mis tarjetas de visita están dentro de mi maletín.
The office staff must check their work schedule daily.
El personal de la oficina debe verificar su horario de trabajo diariamente.
I am going to buy office furniture.
Voy a comprar muebles de oficina.
There isn't any ink in this pen.
No hay tinta en este bolígrafo.
This pencil is missing an eraser.
A este lápiz le falta un borrador.
Our days off are written on the calendar.
Nuestros días libres están escritos en el calendario.
I need to buy extra office supplies.
Necesito comprar suministros adicionales de oficina.
I am busy until my lunch break.
Estoy ocupado hasta mi pausa de almuerzo.

Laptop - Ordenador portátil / computadora portátil
Computer - Computadora / ordenador
Keyboard - Teclado
Mouse - Ratóncito
Email - Correo electrónico / e-mail
Password - Contraseña
Attachment - Adjunto archivo
Printer - Impresora
Colored printer - Impresora a color
To download - Descargar
To upload - Cargar
Internet - Internet
Account - Cuenta
A copy - Copia / **To copy** - Copiar
Cut and paste - Cortar y pegar
Fax - Fax
Scanner - Escáner / **To scan** - Escanear
Telephone - Teléfono
Charger - Cargador / **To charge** - Cargar

I have to write an important email but I forgot my password for my account.
Tengo que escribir un correo electrónico importante pero olvidé la contraseña de mi cuenta.
I need to purchase a computer, a keyboard, a printer, and a desk.
Necesito comprar una computadora, un teclado, una impresora y un escritorio.
Where is the mouse on my laptop?
¿Dónde está el ratóncito en mi computadora portátil?
The internet is slow today therefore it's difficult to upload or download.
Hoy el Internet esta lento, por lo tanto, es difícil de cargar o descargar.
Do you have a colored printer?
¿Tienes una impresora a color?
I needed to fax the contract but instead, I decided to send it as an attachment in the email.
Necesitaba enviar el contrato por fax, pero decidí enviarlo como un archivo adjunto al correo electrónico.
One day, the fax machine will be completely obsolete.
Un día, la máquina de fax quedará completamente obsoleta.
Where is my phone charger?
¿Dónde está el cargador de mi teléfono?
The scanner is broken.
El escáner está roto.
The telephone is behind the chair.
El teléfono está detrás de la silla.

Office

Shredder - Trituradora / destructora de documentos
Copy machine - Maquina de copiar
Filing cabinet - Archivador
Paper - Papel **/ Page -** Página
Paperwork - Papeleo
Portfolio - Portafolio
Files - Archivos
Document - Documento
Contract - Contrato
Records - Registros
Archives - Archivos
Deadline - Fecha límite
Binder - Aglutinante
Paper clip - Sujeta papeles
Stapler - Engrapadora **/ Staples -** Grapas
Stamp - Sello
Mail - Correo
Letter - Carta
Envelope - Sobre
Data - Dato / informacion
Analysis - Análisis
Highlighter - Resaltador **/ Marker -** Marcador **/ To highlight -** Resaltar
Ruler - Regla

The supervisor at our company is responsible for data analysis.
El supervisor de nuestra empresa es responsable del análisis de datos.
The copy machine is next to the telephone.
La copiadora está al lado del teléfono.
The ruler is next to the shredder.
La regla está al lado de la trituradora.
I can't find my stapler, paper clips, nor my highlighter in my cubicle.
No puedo encontrar mi grapadora, clips de papel, ni mi marcador en mi cubículo.
The filing cabinet is full of documents.
El archivador está lleno de documentos.
The garbage can is full of papers.
El basurero está lleno de papeles.
Give me the file because today is the deadline.
Dame el archivo porque hoy es la fecha límite.
Where do I put the binder?
¿Dónde pongo la carpeta?
I need a stamp and an envelope.
Necesito un sello y un sobre.
There is a letter in the mail.
Hay una carta en el correo.

SCHOOL - ESCUELA

Student - Estudiante
Teacher - Profesor / **(f)** profesora, maestro / **(f)** maestra
Substitute teacher - Profesor sustituto / **(f)** Profesor sustituta
A class - Una clase
A classroom - Un aula
Education - Educación
Private school - Escuela privada
Public school - Escuela publica
Elementary school - Escuela primaria
Middle school - Escuela intermedia
High school - Escuela secundaria
University - Universidad / **College -** Colegio
Grade (level) **-** Grado / **Grade** (grade on a test) **-** Calificacione / nota
Pass - Pasó / **Fail -** Falló
Absent - Ausente / **Present -** Presente

The classroom is empty.
El aula está vacía.
I want to bring my laptop to class today.
Quiero llevar mi computadora portátil a la clase hoy.
Our math teacher is absent and therefore a substitute teacher replaced him.
Nuestro professor de matemáticas está ausente, y por lo tanto, un profesor sustituto lo reemplazó.
All the students are present.
Todos los estudiantes están presentes.
Make sure to pass your classes because you can't fail this semester.
Asegúrate de aprobar tus clases porque no puedes reprobar este semestre.
The education level at a private school is much more intense.
El nivel educativo en una escuela privada es mucho más intenso.
I went to a public elementary and middle school.
Fui a la escuela primaria y escuela secundaria pública.
I have good memories of high school.
Tengo buenos recuerdos de la escuela secundaria.
You must get good grades on your report card.
Debe obtener buenas calificaciones en su boleta de calificaciones.
My son is 15 years old and he is in the ninth grade.
Mi hijo tiene 15 años y está en noveno grado.
College textbooks are expensive.
Los libros de texto universitarios son caros.
I want to study at an out-of-state university.
Quiero estudiar en una universidad fuera del estado.

Subject - Tema
Science - Ciencias / **Chemistry -** Química / **Physics -** Física
Geography - Geografía
History - Historia
Math - Matemáticas
Addition - Adición
Subtraction - Sustracción
Division - División
Multiplication - Multiplicación
Language - Idioma / **English -** Inglés / **Foreign language -** Idiomas extranjeros
Physical education - Educación Física
Chalk - Tiza / **Board -** Pizarra
Report card - Boleta de calificaciones
Alphabet - Alfabeto / **Letters -** Letras / **Words -** Palabras
To review - A revisar
Dictionary - Diccionario
Detention - Detención
The principle - El director de la escuela

At school, geography is my favorite subject, English is easy, math is hard, and history is boring.
En la escuela, la geografía es mi materia favorita, el inglés es fácil, las matemáticas son difíciles y la historia es aburrida.
After English class, there is physical education.
Después de la clase de inglés, hay classe de educación física.
Today's math lesson is on addition and subtraction. Next month it will be division and multiplication.
La lección de matemáticas de hoy es sobre suma y resta. El próximo mes será división y multiplicación.
This year for foreign language credits, I want to choose Spanish and French.
Este año para créditos en idiomas extranjeros, quiero elegir español y francés.
I want to buy a dictionary, thesaurus, and a journal for school.
Quiero comprar un diccionario, un diccionario de sinónimos y un periodíco para la escuela.
The teacher needs to write the homework on the board with chalk.
El maestro necesita escribir la tarea en la pizarra con tiza.
Today the students have to review the letters of the alphabet
Hoy los estudiantes tienen que revisar las letras del alfabeto.
The teacher wants to teach roman numerals.
El profesor quiere enseñar los números romanos.
If you can't behave then you must go to the principal's office, and maybe stay after school for detention.
Si no puede comportarse, entonces debe ir a la oficina del director y tal vez quedarse después de la escuela por detención.

School

Test - Examen **/ Quiz -** Prueba / cuestionario
Lesson - Lección **/ Notes -** Notas
Homework - Tarejas, deberes **/ Assignment -** Asignación **/ Project -** Proyecto
Pencil - Lápiz **/ Pen -** Bolígrafo **/ Ink -** Tinta **/ Eraser -** Borrador
Backpack - Mochila
Book - Libro **/ Folders -** Carpetas **/ Notebook -** Cuaderno **/ Papers -** Papeles
Calculator - Calculadora
Glue - Pegamento / cola **/ Scissors -** Tijeras
Adhesive tape - Cinta adhesiva
Lunchbox - Caja de almuerzo **/ Lunch -** Almuerzo **/ Cafeteria -** Cafetería
Kindergarten - Jardín de infancia **/ Pre-school -** Preescolar **/ Day care -** Guardería
Triangle - Triángulo **/ Square -** Cuadrado **/ Circle -** Circulo
Crayons - Lápices de color

Today, we don't have a test but we have a surprise quiz.
Hoy no tenemos un examen, pero tenemos una prueba de sorpresa.
Are a pen, a pencil, and an eraser included with the school supplies?
¿Se incluyen un bolígrafo, un lápiz y un borrador con los útiles escolares?
I think my notepad and calculator are in my backpack.
Creo que mis notas y mi calculadora están en mi mochila.
All my papers are in my folder.
Todos mis papeles están en mi carpeta.
I need glue and scissors for my project.
Necesito pegamento y tijeras para mi proyecto.
I need tape and a stapler to fix my book.
Necesito cinta adhesiva y una grapadora para arreglar mi libro.
You have to concentrate in order to take notes.
Tienes que concentrarte para tomar notas.
The school librarian wants to invite the art and music teacher to the library next week.
El bibliotecario de la escuela quiere invitar al maestro de arte y música a la biblioteca la próxima semana.
For lunch, your children can purchase food at the cafeteria or they can bring food from home.
Para el almuerzo, sus hijos pueden comprar comida en la cafetería o pueden traer comida de casa.
I forgot my lunchbox and crayons at home.
Olvidé mi bolsa de almuerzo y mis crayones en casa.
To draw shapes such as a triangle, square, circle, and rectangle is easy.
Dibujar formas como un triángulo, un cuadrado, un círculo y un rectángulo son fácil.
During the week, my youngest child is at daycare, my middle one is in pre-school, and the oldest is in kindergarten.
Durante la semana, mi hijo menor está en la guardería, mi hijo medino está en la preescolar y el mayor es en la guardería.

PROFESSION - PROFESIÓN

Doctor - Doctor / **(f)** doctora / **Nurse -** Enfermero / **(f)** enfermera
Psychologist - Psicólogo, **(f)** psicóloga / **Psychiatrist -** Psiquiatra, **(f)** psiquiatra
Veterinarian - Veterinario / **(f)** veterinaria
Lawyer - Abogado / abogada / **Judge -** Un juez / **(f)** una jueza
Pilot - Piloto / **Flight attendant -** Azafata
Reporter - Periodista / **Journalist -** Journalista
Electrician - Electricista / **Mechanic -** Mecánico
Investigator - Investigador, **(f)** investigadora / **Detective -** El detective, **(f)** la detective
Translator - Traductor / **(f)** traductora
Producer - Productor / **Director -** Director
Astronaut - Astronauta

What's your profession?
¿Cuál es tu profesión?
I am going to medical school to study medicine because I want to be a doctor.
Voy a la escuela de medicina para estudiar medicina porque quiero ser un médico.
There is a difference between a psychologist and a psychiatrist.
Hay una diferencia entre un psicólogo y un psiquiatra.
Most children want to be an astronaut, a veterinarian, or an athlete.
La mayoría de los niños quieren ser astronautas, veterinarios o atletas.
The judge spoke to the lawyer at the court house.
El juez habló con el abogado en el juzgado.
The police investigator needs to investigate this case.
El investigador policial necesita investigar este caso.
Being a detective could be a fun job.
Ser detective podría ser un trabajo divertido.
The flight attendant and the pilot are on the plane.
La azafata y el piloto están en el avión.
I am a certified electrician.
Soy un electricista certificado.
The mechanic overcharged me.
El mecánico me sobrecargó.
I want to be a journalist.
Quiero ser periodista.
The best translators work at my company.
Los mejores traductores trabajan en mi empresa.
Are you a photographer?
¿Es usted un fotógrafo?
The author wants to hire a ghostwriter to write his book.
El autor quiere contratar a un escritor de fantasmas para que escriba su libro.
I want to find the directors of the company.
Quiero encontrar a los directores de la empresa.

Artist (performer) **-** Artista / ejecutante
Artist (draws paints picture) **-** Artista / dijubador
Author - Autor / **(f)** autora
Painter - Pintor / **(f)** pintora
Dancer - Bailarín / **(f)** bailarina
Writer - Escritor / **(f)** escritora
Photographer - Fotógrafo / **(f)** fótografa
A cook - Un cocinero / **(f)** una cocinera
Waiter - Camarero / **(f)** camarera
Bartender - Camarero de bar / **(f)** camarera de bar
Barber - Peluquero / **Barber shop -** La peluqueria, la barbería
Stylist - Estilista
Maid - Mucama
Caretaker - Vigilante
Farmer - Campesino / granjero
Gardner - Jardinero
Mailman - Cartero
A guard - Un guardia
A cashier - Un cajero / **(f)** una cajera

The artist drew a sketch.
El artista dibujó un boceto.
The artist produced new artwork for her catalog.
La artista produjo nueva obra de arte para su catálogo.
I want to apply as a cook at the restaurant instead of as a waiter.
Quiero postularme como cocinero en el restaurante en lugar de camarero.
The gardener can only come on weekdays.
El jardinero solo puede venir de lunes a viernes.
I have to go to the barbershop now.
Tengo que ir ala peluquería ahora.
Being a bartender isn't an easy job.
Ser cantinero no es un trabajo fácil.
Why do we need another maid?
¿Por qué necesitamos otra criada?
I need to file a complaint against the mailman.
Necesito presentar una queja contra el cartero.
I am a part-time painter.
Soy pintor a tiempo parcial.
She was a dancer at the play.
Ella era una bailarina en la obra de teatro.
You need to contact the insurance company if you want to find another caretaker.
Debe comunicarse con la compañía de seguros si desea encontrar otro cuidador.
The farmer can sell us ripened tomatoes today.
El campesino puede vendernos tomates maduros hoy.

BUSINESS - NEGOCIO

A business - La empresa, negocio / **Company -** Empresa / **Factory -** Fábrica
A professional - Un profesional
Position - Posición / **Work, job -** Trabajo
Employee - Empleado / **(f)** empleada
Manager - Gerente / **Management -** Administración
Owner - Propietario, **(f)** propietaria / dueño, **(f)** dueña
Secretary - Secretario / **(f)** secretaria
An interview - Una entrevista / **Résumé -** Un currículum
Presentation - Presentación
Specialist - Especialista
To hire - Contratar / **To fire -** Despedir
Pay check - Cheque de pago / **Income -** Ingresos / **Salary -** Salario
Insurance - Seguro / **Benefits -** Beneficios
Trimester - Trimestre / **Budget -** Presupuesto
Net - Neto / **Gross -** Bruto
To retire - Jubilar / **Pension -** Pensión, jubilación

I need a job.
Necesito un trabajo.
She is the secretary of the company.
Ella es la secretaria de la empresa.
The manager needs to hire another employee.
El gerente tiene que contratar otro empleado.
I am lucky because I have an interview for a cashier position today.
Tengo suerte porque hoy tengo una entrevista para un puesto de cajero.
How much is the salary and does it include benefits?
¿Cuánto es el salario e incluye beneficios?
Management has your résumé and they need to show it to the owner of the company.
La administración tiene su currículum y deben mostrárselo al propietario de la empresa.
I am at work at the factory now.
Estoy trabajando en la fábrica ahora.
In business, you should be professional.
En los negocios, debes ser profesional.
Is the presentation ready?
¿Está lista la presentación?
The first trimester is part of the annual budget.
El primer trimestre es parte del presupuesto anual.
I have to see the net and gross profits of the business.
Tengo que ver las ganancias netas y brutas del negocio.
I want to retire already.
Quiero jubilarme ya.

Client - Cliente
Broker - Agente / corredor / **Salesperson** - Vendedor / **(f)** vendedora
Realtor - Agente inmobiliario / **(f)** agente inmobiliaria
Real estate - Inmobiliario / **Real estate agency** - Agencia inmobiliaria
A purchase - Una compra / **A lease** - Un arrendamiento / **To lease** - Arrendar
To invest - Invertir / **Investment** - Inversión / **Investor** - Inversor
Economy - Economía
Mortgage - Hipoteca / **Interest rate** - Tasa de interés / **A loan** - Un préstamo
Commission - Comisión / **Percent** - Por ciento
A sale - Una venta / **Profit** - Lucro, ganancia, beneficio / **Value** - Valor
Landlord - Dueño, **(f)** dueña / **Tenant** - Inquilino, **(f)** inquilina
The demand - La demanda / **The supply** - El suministro
A contract - Un contrato / **Terms** - Términos / **Signature** - Firma / **Initials** - Iniciales
Stocks - Acciones / **Stock broker** - Agente de bolsa
Advertisement - Publicidad / **Ads** - Anuncios

I can earn a huge profit from stocks.
Puedo obtener grandes ganancias de las acciones.
The demand in the real estate market depends on the economy.
La demanda en el mercado inmobiliario depende de la economía.
If you want to sell your home, I can recommend a very good realtor.
Si desea vender su casa, le puedo recomendar un muy buen agente inmobiliario.
The investor wants to invest in this shopping center because he says it has good potential.
El inversor quiere invertir en este centro comercial porque dice que tiene un buen potencial.
The value of the property increased by twenty percent.
El valor de la propiedad aumentó en un veinte por ciento.
How much is the commission on the sale?
¿Cuánto es la comisión por la venta?
The client wants to lease instead of purchasing the property.
El cliente quiere arrendar en lugar de comprar la propiedad.
What are the terms of the purchase?
¿Cuáles son los términos de la compra?
I can negotiate a better interest rate.
Puedo negociar una mejor tasa de intereses.
I need a small loan in order to pay my mortgage this month.
Necesito un pequeño préstamo para pagar mi hipoteca este mes.
I need a signature and an initial on the contract.
Necesito una firma y una inicial en el contrato.
My position in the company is marketing and I am responsible for advertising and ads.
Mi posición en la empresa es "marketing" y soy responsable de la publicidad y los anuncios.

Business

Money - Dinero / **Currency** - Moneda
Cash - Efectivo / **Coins** - Monedas
Change (change for a bill) - Cambio
Credit - Crédito
Tax - Impuesto
Price - Precio
Invoice - Factura
Inventory - Inventario
Merchandise - Mercancías
A refund - Un reembolso
Product - Producto
Produced - Producido
Retail - Al por menor
Wholesale - Venta al por mayor
Imports - Importaciones / **Exports** - Exportaciones
To ship - Envíar
Shipment - Envío

Don't forget to bring cash with you.
No olvide traer efectivo con usted.
Do you have change for a $100 bill?
¿Tiene usted cambio para una billete de cien dolares?
I don't have a credit card.
No tengo tarjeta de crédito.
The salesperson told me there is no refund.
El vendedor me dijo que no hay reembolso.
This product is produced in Italy.
Este producto se produce en Italia.
I work in the export/import business.
Trabajo en el negocio de exportación y importación.
Let me check my inventory.
Déjame revisar mi inventario.
This product is covered by insurance.
Este producto está cubierto por el seguro.
This invoice contains a mistake.
Esta factura contiene un error.
What is the wholesale and retail value of this shipment?
¿Cuál es el valor mayorista y minorista de este envío?
You don't have enough money to purchase the merchandise.
No tienes suficiente dinero para comprar la mercancía.
How much does the shipping cost and is it in US currency?
¿Cuánto cuesta el envío y es en moneda estadounidense?
There is a tax exemption on this income.
Hay una extensión de impuestos sobre este ingreso.

SPORTS - DEPORTES

Basketball - Baloncesto / **Soccer -** Fútbol / **Baseball -** Béisbol
Game - Juego / **Stadium -** Estadio / **Ball -** Pelota
Player - Un jugador / **(f)** una jugadora
To jump - Saltar / **To throw -** Tirar / **To kick -** Patear / **To catch -** Atrapar
Coach - Entrenador / **(f)** entrenadora / **Referee -** Árbitro
Competition - Competencia
Team - Equipo / grupo / **Teammate -** Compañero de equipo
National team - Selección nacional
Opponent - Adversario
Half time - Medio tiempo / **Finals -** Finales
Score - Puntuación / **Scores -** Puntajes
Goal - Objetivo / **The goal -** La meta
To lose - Perder / **A Defeat -** Una derrota / **To win -** Ganar / **A victory -** Una victoria
The looser - El perdedor / **The winner -** El ganador
Fans - Aficionados
Field - Campo
Helmet - Casco / **Basket -** Cesta
A whistle - Un silbato
Penalty - Multa / pena

I like to watch basketball games.
Me gusta ver juegos de baloncesto.
Soccer is my favorite sport.
El fútbol es mi deporte favorito
I have tickets to a football game at the stadium.
Tengo boletos para un juego de fútbol americano en el estadio.
To play basketball, you need to be good at shooting and jumping.
Para jugar baloncesto, debes de ser bueno en disparar y saltar.
The national team has a lot of fans.
El equipo nacional tiene muchos aficionados.
My teammate can't find his baseball helmet.
Mi compañero de equipo no puede encontrar su casco de béisbol.
The coach and the team were on the field during half-time.
El entrenador y el equipo estuvieron en el campo durante el descanso.
The coach needs to bring his team today to meet the new referee.
El entrenador necesita traer a su equipo hoy para conocer al nuevo árbitro.
Our opponents went home after their defeat.
Nuestros oponentes se fueron a casa después de su derrota.
The player received a penalty for kicking the ball in the wrong goal.
El jugador recibió una penalización por patear la pelota en la portería equivocada.
Not every person likes sports.
No a todas las personas les gustan los deportes.

Athlete - El deportista / **(f)** la deportista
Olympics - Juegos Olímpicos / **World cup** - Copa Mundial
Bicycle - Bicicleta / **Cyclist** - Ciclista / **Swimming** - Natación
Wrestling - Lucha / **Boxing** - Boxeo / **Martial arts** - Artes marciales
Championship - Campeonato / **Award** - Premio / **Tournament** - Torneo
Horse racing - Las carreras de caballos / **Racing** - Carreras
Pool (billiards) - Billar / **Pool** (swimming pool) - Piscina
Exercise - Ejercicio / **Fitness** - Aptitud / **Gym** - Gimnasio
Captain - Capitán / **Judge** - Juez, **(f)** jueza
A match - Un combate / **Rules** - Reglas / **Track** - Pista
Trainer - Entrenador / **(f)** entrenadora

Today are the finals for the Olympic Games.
Hoy son las finales de los Juegos Olímpicos.
Let's see who wins the World Cup.
Veamos quién gana el Mundial.
I want to compete in the cycling championship.
Quiero competir en el campeonato de ciclismo.
I am an athlete so I must stay in shape.
Soy un atleta, así que debo mantenerme en forma.
After my boxing lesson, I want to go and swim in the pool.
Después de mi clase de boxeo, quiero ir a nadar a la piscina.
He will receive an award because he is the winner of the martial-arts tournament.
Recibirá un premio porque es el ganador del torneo de artes marciales.
The wrestling captain must teach his team the rules of the sport.
El capitán de lucha debe enseñar a su equipo las reglas del deporte.
At the horse-racing competition, the judge couldn't announce the score.
En la competencia de carreras de caballos, el juez no pudo anunciar el puntaje.
There is a bicycle race at the park today.
Hoy hay una carrera de bicicletas en el parque.
This fitness program is expensive.
Este programa de ejercicios es costoso.
It's healthy to go to the gym every day.
Es saludable ir al gimnasio todos los días.
Weightlifting is good exercise.
El levantamiento de pesas es un buen ejercicio.
I want to run on the track today.
Quiero correr en la pista hoy.
I like to win in billiards.
Me encanta ganar en juego de billiard.
Skateboarding is forbidden here.
El skateboard está prohibido aquí.
Skating is much easier than it seems.
Patinar es mucho más fácil de lo que parece.

OUTDOOR ACTIVITIES - ACTIVIDADES AL AIRE LIBRE

Hiking - Excursionismo
Hiking trail - Ruta de senderismo
Pocket knife - Cuchillo de bolsillo
Compass - Brújula
Camping - Campamento
RV - Casa rodante
Campground - Terreno de campamento
Tent - Tienda
Campfire - Hoguera, fogata / **Matches -** Fósforos / **Lighter -** Encendedor
Coal - Carbón
Flame - Fuego
The smoke - El humo
Fishing / to fish - Pescar
Fishing pole - Caña de pesca / **Fishing line -** Línea de pesca / sedal
Hook - Gancho / **A float -** Flotador/ **A weight -** Peso / **Bait -** Cebo
Fishing net - Red de pescar
To hunt - Cazar
Rifle - Rifle / escopeta

I enjoy hiking on the trail, with my compass and my pocketknife.
Me encanta ir de excursión por el sendero, con mi brújula y mi navaja.
Don't forget the water bottle in your backpack.
No olvides de poner la botella de agua en tu mochilla.
There aren't any tents at the campground.
No hay tiendas de campaña en el campamento.
I want to sleep in an RV instead of a tent.
Quiero dormir en una casa rodante en vez de una tienda.
We can use a lighter to start a campfire.
Podemos usar un encendedor para iniciar una fogata.
We need coal and matches for the camping trip.
Necesitamos carbón y fósforos para el viaje de campamento.
Put out the fire because the flames are very high and there is a lot of smoke.
Apague el fuego porque las llamas son muy altas y hay mucho humo.
There is fog outside and the temperature is below freezing.
Hay neblina afuera y la temperatura esta en bajo cero.
Where is the fishing store? I need to buy hooks, fishing line, bait, and a net.
¿Dónde está la tienda de pesca? Necesito comprar ganchos, sedal, cebo y una red.
You can't bring your fishing pole or your hunting rifle to the campground of the State Park because there is a sign there which says, "No fishing and no hunting."
No puede llevar su caña de pesca o su rifle de caza al campamento del Parque Estatal. Porque hay el letrero dice: "No pescar ni cazar".

Sailing - Navegación
A sail - Una vela
Sailboat - Velero
Rowing - Remo
A paddle - Un remo
Motor - Motor
Canoe - Canoa
Kayak - Kayac
Rock climbing - Escalada de roca
Horseback riding - Cabalgatas
Diver - Buceador / (f) buceadora
Scuba diving - Submarinismo
Skydiving - Paracaidismo
Parachute - Paracaídas
Paragliding - Parapente
Hot air balloon - Globo aerostático
Kite - Una cometa
Surfing - Surf
Surf board - Tabla de surf
Ice skating - Patinaje sobre hielo / **Skiing** - Esquiar

With a broken motor, we need a paddle to row the boat.
Con el motor roto, necesitamos una rema para remar el bote.
It's important to know how to use a sail before sailing on a sailboat.
Es importante saber cómo usar una vela antes de navegar en un velero.
In my opinion, a kayak is much more fun than a canoe.
En mi opinión, un kayak es mucho más divertido que una canoa.
Do I need to bring my scuba certification in order to scuba dive at the reef?
¿Necesito traer mi certificación de buceo para bucear en el arrecife?
I have my mask, snorkel, and fins.
Tengo mi máscara, snorkel y aletas.
I don't know which is scarier, sky diving or paragliding.
No sé cuál es más aterrador, paracaidismo o parapente.
There are several outdoor activities here including rock climbing and horseback riding.
Aquí hay varias actividades al aire libre, como escalada en roca y paseos a caballo.
My dream was always to fly in a hot-air balloon.
Mi sueño siempre fue volar en un globo aerostático.
We are going skiing on our next vacation.
Vamos a esquiar en nuestras próxima vacacion.
Where is the surfboard? I want to surf the waves at the beach tomorrow.
¿Dónde está la tabla de surf? Quiero surfear las olas en la playa mañana.
Ice skating is fun.
El patinaje sobre hielo es divertido.

ELECTRICAL DEVICES - APARATOS ELÉCTRICOS

Electric - Eléctrico **/ Electricity -** Electricidad **/ Electronic -** Electrónica
Appliance - Aparato / electrodoméstico
Oven - Horno
Stove - Estufa
Microwave - Microondas
Refrigerator - Refrigerador **/ Freezer -** Congelador
Coffee maker - Maquina de cafe / **Coffee pot-** Cafetera
Toaster - Tostadora
Dishwasher - Lavavajillas
Laundry machine - Lavadora **/ Laundry -** Lavandería
Dryer - Secadora
Fan - Ventilador **/ Air condition -** Aire acondicionado
Alarm - Alarma **/ Smoke detector -** Detector de humo
Remote control - Control remoto
Battery - Batería

He needs to pay his electric bill if he wants electricity.
Necesita pagar su factura de electricidad si quiere electricidad.
I need to purchase a few things at the electronic store and at the appliance store tomorrow.
Necesito comprar algunas cosas en la tienda electrónica y en la tienda de electrodomésticos mañana.
I can't put plastic utensils in the dishwasher.
No puedo poner utensilios de plástico en el lavavajillas.
I am going to get rid of my microwave and oven because they are not functioning.
Me voy a deshacer de mi microondas y mi horno porque no funcionan.
The refrigerator and freezer aren't cold enough.
El refrigerador y el congelador no están suficientemente fríos.
The coffee maker and toaster are in the kitchen.
La machina de cafe y la tostadora están en la cocina.
My washing machine and dryer do not function therefore I must wash my laundry at the public laundromat.
Mi lavadora y secadora no funcionan, así que tal vez tengo que lavar mi ropa en la lavandería.
Is this fan new?
¿Es este ventilador nuevo?
Unfortunately, the new air conditioner unit hasn't been delivered yet.
Desafortunadamente, la nueva unidad de aire acondicionado aún no se ha entregado.
Is that annoying sound the alarm clock or the fire alarm?
¿Es ese molesto sonido el despertador o la alarma de incendio?
The smoke detector needs new batteries.
El detector de humo necesita baterías.

Lamp - Lámpara
Stereo - Estéreo
A clock / a watch - Un reloj
Vacuum cleaner - Aspiradora
Phone - Teléfono
Text message - Mensaje de texto / **Voicemail** - Mensaje de voz
Camera - Cámara
Flashlight - Linterna / **Light** - Luz
Furnace - Horno / **Heater** - Calentador
Cord - Cordón / **Charger** - Cargador
Outlet - Enchufe
Headsets - Auriculares
Door bell - Timbre de la puerta
Lawn mower - Cortacésped

The clock is hanging on the wall.
El reloj está colgado en la pared.
The cordless stereo is on the table.
El estéreo inalámbrico está sobre la mesa.
I still have a home telephone.
Todavía tengo un teléfono de casa.
I need to buy a lamp and a vacuum cleaner today.
Necesito comprar una lámpara y una aspiradora hoy.
In the past, cameras were more common. Today, everyone can use their phones to take pictures.
En el pasado, las cámaras eran más comunes. Hoy, todos pueden usar sus teléfonos para tomar fotos.
You can leave me a voicemail or send me a text message.
Puedes dejarme un mensaje de voz o enviarme un mensaje de texto.
The lights don't function when there is a blackout therefore I must rely on my flashlight.
Las luces no funcionan cuando hay un apagón, por eso, debo confiar en mi linterna.
I can't hear the doorbell.
No puedo escuchar el timbre.
There is a higher risk of causing a house fire from an electric heater than a furnace.
Existe un mayor riesgo de provocar un incendio en la casa de un calentador eléctrico que un horno.
I need to connect the cord to the outlet.
Necesito conectar el cable al enchufe.
His lawnmower is very noisy.
Su cortadora de césped es muy ruidosa.
Why is my headset on the floor?
¿Por qué mi auricular está en el suelo?

TOOLS - HERRAMIENTAS

Toolbox - Caja de herramientas
Carpenter - Carpintero
Hammer - Martillo
Saw - Sierra **/ Axe -** Hacha
A drill - Perforador / **To drill -** Perforar
Nail - Clavo **/ A screw -** Un tornillo
Screwdriver - Destornillador **/ Pliers -** Alicates **/ Wrench -** Llave inglesa
Paint brush - Cepillo de pintura **/ To paint -** Pintar **/ The paint -** La pintura
Ladder - Escalera
Rope - Cuerda **/ String -** Cuerda
A scale - Una escala **/ Measuring tape -** Cinta métrica
Machine - Máquina
A lock - Candado **/ Locked -** Cerrada **/ To lock -** Cerrar
Equipment - Equipo
Metal - Metal **/ Steel -** Acero **/ Iron -** Hierro
Broom - Escoba **/ Dust pan -** El recogedor
Mop - Esponja / trapo / fregona
Bucket - Cubo **/ Sponge -** Esponja
Shovel - Pala **/ A trowel -** Una paleta

The carpenter needs nails, a hammer, a saw, and a drill.
El carpintero necesita clavos, un martillo, una sierra y un taladro.
The string is very long. Where are the scissors?
La cuerda es muy larga. ¿Dónde están las tijeras?
The screwdriver is in the toolbox.
El destornillador está en la caja de herramientas.
This tool can cut through metal.
Esta herramienta puede cortar metal.
The ladder is next to the tools.
La escalera está al lado de las herramientas.
I must buy a brush to paint the walls.
Debo comprar un pincel para pintar las paredes.
The paint bucket is empty
El cubo de pintura está vacío.
It's better to tie the shovel with a rope in my truck.
Es mejor atar la pala con una soga en mi camioneta.
How can I fix this machine?
¿Cómo puedo arreglar esta máquina?
The broom and dust pan are with the rest of my cleaning equipment.
La escoba y el recogedor están con el resto de mi equipo de limpieza.
Where did you put the mop and the bucket?
¿Dónde pusiste el trapo y el cubo?

CAR - AUTO

Engine - Motor
Ignition - Ignición
Steering wheel - Volante
Automatic - Automático
Manual - Manual
Gear shift - Palanca de cambios / cambio de marchas
Seat - Asiento
Seat belt - Cinturón de seguridad
Airbag - Bolsa de aire
Brakes - Frenos
Hand brake - Freno de mano
Baby seat - Asiento de bebe
Driver seat - Asiento del conductor
Passenger seat - Asiento del pasajero
Front seat - Siento delantero
Back seat - Asiento trasero
Car passenger - Pasajero del coche
Warning light - Luz de alerta
Button - Botón
Horn (of the car) **-** Bocina

When driving, both hands must be on the steering wheel.
Al conducir, ambas manos deben estar en el volante.
I must take my car to my mechanic because there is a problem with the ignition.
Debo llevar mi automóvil a mi mecánico porque hay un problema con el ignición.
What's happened to the engine?
¿Qué le paso al motor?
The seat is missing a seat belt.
Al asiento le falta el cinturón de seguridad.
I prefer a gear shift instead of an automatic car.
Prefiero un cambio de marcha en lugar de un automóvil automático.
The brakes are new in this vehicle
Los frenos son nuevos en este auto.
This vehicle doesn't have a handbreak.
Este vehiculo no tiene un freno de mano.
There is an airbag on both the driver side and the passenger side.
Hay una bolsa de aire tanto en el lado del conductor como en el lado del pasajero.
The baby seat is in the back seat.
El asiento para bebé está en el asiento trasero.
The warning light button is located next to the stirring wheel.
El botón de la luz de advertencia se encuentra al lado del volante.

Windshield - Parabrisas
Windshield wiper - Limpiaparabrisas
Windshield fluid - Líquido parabrisas
Rear view mirror - Espejo retrovisor
Side mirror - Espejo lateral
Door handle - Manija de la puerta
Spare tire - Llanta de repuesto
Trunk - Maletero
Hood (of the vehicle) - Capó del vehículo
Alarm - Alarma
Window - Ventana
Drive license - Licencia de conducir/manejar
License plate - Placa
Gas - Gasolina
Low fuel - Bajo combustible
Flat tire - Llanta desinflado
Crowbar - Palanca
A jack - Un gato

The windshield and all four of my car windows are cracked.
El parabrisas y las cuatro ventanas de mi auto están agrietados.
I want to clean my rear-view mirror and my side mirrors.
Quiero limpiar mi espejo retrovisor y mis espejos laterales.
My car doesn't have an alarm.
Mi auto no tiene alarma.
Does this car have a spare tire in the trunk?
¿Hay una llanta de repuesto en el maletero de este auto?
Please, close the car door.
Por favor, cierra la puerta del auto.
Where is the nearest gas station?
¿Dónde está la gasolinera más cercana?
The windshield wipers are new.
Los limpiaparabrisas son nuevos.
The door handle on the driver's side is broken.
La manija de la puerta del lado del conductor está rota.
Your license plate has expired.
Su placa ha expirado.
I need to renew my driving license today.
Necesito renovar mi licencia de conducir hoy.
Are the car doors locked?
¿Están las puertas del auto cerradas?

NATURE - NATURALEZA

A plant - Una planta
Forest - Bosque
Tree - Árbol / **Wood -** Madera
Trunk - Tronco / **Branch -** Rama / **Leaf -** Hoja / **Root -** Raíz
Flowers - Flores
Petal - Pétalo
Blossom - Florecer
Stem - Tallo / **Seed -** Semilla
Rose - Rosa
Nectar - Néctar / **Pollen -** Polen
Vegetation - Vegetación / **Bush -** Arbusto / **Grass -** Césped
Rain forest - Selva / **Tropical -** Tropical
Palm tree - Palmera / palma
Season - Estaciones del ano
Spring - Primavera / **Summer -** Verano / **Winter -** Invierno / **Autumn -** Otoño

I want to collect a few leaves during the fall.
Quiero recoger algunas hojas durante el otoño.
There aren't any plants in the desert during this season.
No hay plantas en el desierto durante esta temporada.
The trees need rain.
Los árboles necesitan lluvia.
The trunk, the branches, and the roots are all parts of the tree.
El tronco, las ramas y las raíces son todas partes del árbol.
Palm trees can only grow in a tropical climate.
Las palmeras solo pueden crecer en un clima tropical.
My rose bushes are beautiful.
Mis rosales son hermosos.
Where can I plant the seeds?
¿Dónde puedo plantar las semillas?
I must cut the grass and vegetation in my garden.
Debo cortar el césped y la vegetación en mi jardín.
The rain forest is a nature preserve.
La selva tropical es una reserva natural.
I am allergic to pollen.
Soy alérgico/(f) alérgica al polen.
The orchid needs to bloom because I want to see its beautiful petals.
La orquídea tiene que florecer porque quiero ver sus hermosos pétalos.
Is the nectar from the flower sweet?
¿Es el néctar de la flor dulce?
Be careful because the plant stem can break very easily.
Tenga cuidado porque el tallo de la planta puede romperse muy fácilmente.

Lake - Lago
Sea - Mar
Ocean - Oceano
Waterfall - Cascada / cataratas
River - Río / **Canal -** Canal / **Swamp -** Pantano
Mountain - Montaña / **Hill -** Colina / **Cliff -** Acantilado / **Peak -** Pico
Rainbow - Arco iris
Clouds - Nubes
Lightning - Relámpago / **Thunder -** Trueno
Rain - Lluvia / **Snow -** Nieve
Ice - Hielo / **Hail -** Granizo
Fog - Neblina
Wind - Viento / **Air -** Aire
Dawn - Amanecer / **Dew -** Rocío
Sunset - Crepúsculo / **Sunrise -** Alba / salida del sol

There is a rainbow above the waterfall.
Hay un arco iris encima de la cascada.
The ocean is bigger than the sea.
El océano es más grande que el mar.
From the mountain, I can see the river.
Desde la montaña, puedo ver el río.
Today we hope to see snow.
Hoy esperamos ver la nieve.
There aren't any clouds in the sky.
No hay nubes en el cielo.
I see the lightning from my window.
Veo el relámpago desde mi ventana.
I can hear the thunder from outside.
Puedo escuchar el trueno de afuera.
I want to see the sunset from the hill.
Quiero ver el crepúsculo desde la colina.
The lake has a shallow part and a deep part.
El lago tiene una parte poco profunda y una parte profunda.
I don't like the wind.
No me gusta el viento.
The air on the mountain is very clear.
El aire en la montaña esta muy claro.
Every dawn, there is dew on the leaves of my plants.
En cada amanecer, hay rocío en las hojas de mis plantas.
Is this ice or hail?
¿Es esto hielo o granizo?
 I can see the volcano.
Puedo ver el volcan.

Nature

Sky - Cielo
World - Mundo
Earth / ground / soil - Tierra
Sun - Sol / **Moon** - Luna / **Crescent** - Creciente / **Star** - Estrella / **Planet** - Planeta
Fire - Fuego / **Heat** - Calor / **Humidity** - Humedad
Field - Campo
Agriculture - Agricultura
Weeds - Malas hierbas
Island - Isla
Cave - Cueva / caverna
Park - Parque / **National park** - Parque nacional
Rock - Roca / **Stone** - Piedra
Sea shore - Orilla del mar / **Seashell** - Concha
Dawn - Amanecer
Ray - Rayo
Dry - Seco / **Wet** - Mojado
Deep - Profundo / **Shallow** - Poco profundo
A stick - Un palo
Dust - Polvo

The moon and the stars are beautiful in the night sky.
La luna y las estrellas son hermosas en el cielo nocturno.
The earth is a planet, and the sun is a star.
La tierra es un planeta y el sol es una estrella.
The heat today is unbearable.
El calor hoy es insoportable.
At the beach there is fresh air.
Hay aire fresco en la playa.
I want to sail to the island to see the sunrise.
Quiero navegar a la isla para ver el amanecer.
Parts of the cave are dry and other parts are wet.
Partes de la cueva están secas y otras partes están mojadas.
We live in a beautiful world.
Vivimos en un mundo hermoso.
There is dust from the fire in the park.
Hay polvo del fuego en el parque.
I want to collect seashells from the seashore.
Quiero recoger conchas de la orilla del mar.
There are too many rocks in the soil so it's impossible to use this area as a field for agricultural purposes.
Hay demasiadas rocas en esta tierra, por eso es imposible utilizar esta área como campo para fines agrícolas.
Why are there so many weeds growing by the swamp?
¿Por qué hay tantas yierbas creciendo junto al pantano?

ANIMALS - ANIMALES

Animals - Animales
Pet - Mascota
Mammal - Mamífero
Cat - Gato / **Dog -** Perro
Parrot - Loro / papagayo
Pigeon - Paloma
Pig - Cerdo
Sheep - Oveja
Cow - Vaca / **Bull -** Toro
Donkey - Burro / **Horse -** Caballo
Camel - Camello
Rodent - Roedor
Mouse - Ratón / **Rat -** Una rata
Rabbit - Conejo / **Hamster -** Hámster
Duck - Pato / **Goose -** Ganso
Turkey - Pavo / **Chicken -** Gallina, **(m)** gallo / **Poultry -** Aves de corral
Squirrel - Ardilla

I have a dog and two cats.
Tengo un perro y dos gatos.
There is a bird on the tree.
Hay un pájaro en el árbol.
I want to go to the zoo to see the animals.
Quiero ir al jardin zoológico para ver a los animales.
My daughter wants a pet horse.
Mi hija quiere un caballo como mascota.
A pig, a sheep, a donkey, and a cow are considered farm animals.
Un cerdo, una oveja, un burro y una vaca se consideran animales de granja.
I want a hamster as a pet.
Quiero un hámster como mascota.
A camel is a desert animal.
Un camello es un animal del desierto.
Can I put ducks, geese, and turkeys inside my chicken coop?
¿Puedo poner patos, gansos y pavos dentro de mi gallinero?
We have rabbits and squirrels in our patio.
Tenemos conejos y ardillas en nuestro patio.
It's cruel to keep a parrot inside a cage.
Es cruel mantener un loro dentro de una jaula.
There are many pigeons in the city.
Hay muchas palomas en la ciudad.
Mice and rats are rodents.
Los ratones y las ratas son roedores.

Lion - León
Hyena - Hiena
Leopard - Leopardo
Panther - Pantera
Cheetah - Guepardo
Elephant - Elefante
Rhinoceros - Rinoceronte
Hippopotamus - Hipopótamo
Bat - Murciélago
Fox - Zorro / **Wolf** - Lobo
Weasel - Comadreja
Bear - Oso
Tiger - Tigre
Deer - Ciervo
Monkey - Mono / (f) mona
Sloth - El mono perezoso
Marsupial - Marsupial

There are a lot of animals in the forest.
Hay muchos animales en el bosque.
The most dangerous animal in Africa is not the lion, it's the hippopotamus.
El animal más peligroso en África no es el león, es el hipopótamo.
A wolf is much bigger than a fox.
Un lobo es mucho más grande que un zorro.
Are there bears in this forest?
¿Hay osos en este bosque?
Bats are the only mammals that can fly.
Los murciélagos son los únicos mamíferos que pueden volar.
It's usually very difficult to see leopards in the wild.
Por lo general, es muy difícil ver leopardos en la naturaleza.
Cheetahs are common in certain regions of Africa.
Los guepardos son comunes en ciertas regiones de África.
Elephants and rhinoceroses are known as very aggressive animals.
Los elefantes y los rinocerontes son conciderados como animales muy agresivos.
I saw a hyena and a panther at the safari yesterday.
Ayer vi una hiena y una pantera en el safari.
The largest member of the cat family is the tiger.
El miembro más grande de la familia de los gatos es el tigre.
Deer hunting is forbidden in the national park.
La caza de ciervos está prohibida en el parque nacional.
There are many monkeys on the branches of the trees.
Hay muchos monos en las ramas de los árboles.
An opossum isn't a rat but it's a marsupial just like the kangaroo.
Una zarigüeya no es una rata, pero es un marsupial al igual que el canguro.

Animals

Bird - Pájaro
Crow - Cuervo
Stork - Cigüeña
Eagle - Águila / **Vulture** - Buitre
Owl - Búho
Peacock - Pavo real
Reptile - Reptil
Turtle - Tortuga
Snake - Serpiente / **Lizard** - Lagartija / **Crocodile** - Cocodrilo
Frog - Rana
Seal - Foca
Whale - Ballena / **Dolphin** - Delfín
Fish - Pescado
Shark - Tiburón
Wing - Ala / **Feather** - Pluma
Tail - Cola
Fur - Piel
Scales - Escamas
Fins - Aletas
Horns - Cuernos
Claws - Garras

Eagles and owls are birds of prey however vultures are scavengers.
Las águilas y los búhos son aves rapaces, sin embargo, los buitres son carroñeros.
Crows are very smart.
Cuervos son muy inteligentes.
I want to see the stork migration in Europe.
Quiero ver la migración de la cigüeña en Europa.
Don't buy a fur coat!
¡No compra un abrigo de piel!
Butterflies and peacocks are colorful.
Las mariposas y los pavos reales son coloridos.
Some snakes are poisonous.
Algunas serpientes son venenosas.
Is that the sound of a cricket or a frog?
¿Es ese el sonido de un grillo o una rana?
Lizards, crocodiles, and turtles belong to the reptile family.
Lagartos, cocodrilos y tortugas pertenecen a la familia de los reptiles.
I want to see the fish in the lake.
Quiero ver los peces en el lago.
There were a lot seals basking on the beach last week.
Muchas focas habían tomando el sol en la playa la semana pasada.
A whale is not a fish.
Una ballena no es un pez.

Insect - Insecto
A cricket - Un grillo
Ant - Hormiga / **Termite -** Termita
A fly - Una mosca
Butterfly - Mariposa
Worm - Gusano
Mosquito - Mosquito / **Flea -** Pulga / **Lice -** Piojo
Beetle - Escarabajo
A roach - Una cucaracha
Bee - Abeja
Spider - Araña
Scorpion - Escorpión
Snail - Caracol
Invertebrates - Invertebrados
Shrimps - Camerones / **Clams -** Almejas / **Crab -** Cangrejo
Octopus - Pulpo
Starfish - Estrella de mar
Jellyfish - Medusa

An octopus has eight tentacles.
El pulpo tiene ocho tentáculos.
Jellyfish is a common dish in Asian culture.
En la cultura asiática la medusa es un plato común.
The museum has a large collection of invertebrate fossils.
El museo tiene una gran colección de fósiles de invertebrados.
I want to buy mosquito spray.
Quiero comprar repelente de mosquitos.
I need antiseptic for my bug bites.
Necesito antiséptico para mis mordizcos de insectos.
I hope there aren't any worms, ants, or flies in the bag of sugar.
Espero que no haya gusanos, hormigas o moscas en la bolsa de azúcar.
I have crabs and starfish in my aquarium.
Tengo cangrejos y estrellas de mar en mi acuario.
Certain types of spiders and scorpions can be dangerous.
Ciertos tipos de arañas y escorpiones pueden ser peligrosos.
I need to call the exterminator because there are fleas, roaches, and termites in my house.
Necesito llamar al exterminador porque hay pulgas, cucarachas y termitas en mi casa.
Bees are very important for the environment.
Las abejas son muy importantes para el medio ambiente.
Is there a snail inside the shell?
¿Hay un caracol dentro del caparazón?
Beetles are my favorite insects.
Los escarabajos son mis insectos favoritos.

RELIGION, HOLIDAYS & TRADITION
RELIGIÓN, FIESTAS Y TRADICIONES

God - Dios / **Bible** - Biblia
Old Testament - Viejo Testamento / **New Testament** - Nuevo Testamento
Adam - Adam / **Eve** - Eva / **Garden of Eden** - Jardín del Edén
Heaven - Cielo / **Angels** - Ángeles
Noah - Noé / **Ark** - Arca
To pray - Orar, rezar / **Prayer** - Oración, un rezo
Blessing - Bendición / **To bless** - Bendecir / **Holy** - Santo / **Faith** - Fe
Moses - Moisés / **Prophet** - Profeta / **Messiah** - Mesías / **Miracle** - Milagro
Ten commandments - Diez Mandamientos
The five books of Moses - Los cinco libros de Moises
Genesis - Génesis / **Exodus** - Éxodo / **Leviticus** - Levítico
Numbers - Números / **Deuteronomy** - Deuteronomio

What is your religion?
¿Cual es tu religion?
Many religions use the chapel.
Muchas religones usan la capilla.
We have faith in miracles.
Tenemos fe en los milagros.
When do I need to say the blessing?
¿Cuándo tengo que decir la bendición?
I must say a prayer for the holiday.
Tengo que decir una oración por las fiestas.
The angels came from heaven.
Los ángeles vinieron del cielo.
Aaron, the brother of Moses, was the first priest.
Aarón, el hermano de Moisés, fue el primer sacerdote.
The story of Noah's Ark and the flood is very interesting.
La historia del Arca de Noé y el diluvio es muy interesante.
Adam and Eve were the first humans and they lived in the Garden of Eden.
Adán y Eva fueron los primeros humanos y vivieron en el Jardín del Edén.
Moses had to climb up on Mount Sinai to receive the Ten Commandments from God.
Moisés tuvo que subir al Monte Sinaí para recibir los Diez Mandamientos de Dios.
The Five Books of the Moses are Genesis, Exodus, Leviticus, Numbers, and Deuteronomy.
Los cinco libros de Moisés son Génesis, Éxodo, Levítico, Números y Deuteronomio.
Moses was considered as the prophet of all prophets.
Moisés fue considerado como el profeta de todos los profetas.
My favorite book of the bible is the Book of Prophets.
Mi libro favorito de la Biblia es el Libro de los Profetas.

Christian Religion - Religión christiano
Church - Iglesia / **Cathedral** - Catedral
Catholic - Católico, **(f)** Católica / **Christian** - Cristiano, **(f)** Cristiana
Christianity - Cristiandad / **Catholicism** - Catolicismo / **Priest** - Sacerdote, padre, cura
A cross - Cruz
Jesus - Jesús
Holy - Santo / **Holy water** - Agua bendita
To sin - Pecar / **A sin** - Un pecado
Monastery - Monasterio
Christmas - Navidad / **Christmas tree** - árbol de Navidad / **Christmas eve** - Nochebuena
New Year - Año nuevo / **Merry Christmas** - Feliz Navidad
Easter - Pascuas
Saint - Santo, **(f)** Santa / **Nun** - Monja
Chapel - Capilla
Hell - Infierno / **Devil** - Diablo / **Demons** - Demonios

The church is open today.
La iglesia está abierta hoy.
Christians love to celebrate Christmas.
A los cristianos les encanta celebrar la Navidad.
I need to turn on the lights on my Christmas tree for Christmas Eve.
Necesito encender las luces de mi árbol de Navidad para la víspera de Navidad.
Two more weeks until Easter.
Dos semanas más hasta las Pascuas.
The nuns live in the monastery.
Las monjas viven en el monasterio.
Jesus is the son of God.
Jesús es el hijo de Dios.
I have a gold necklace with a cross.
Tengo un collar de oro con una cruz.
The priest read the Holy Bible in front of the congregation.
El sacerdote leyó la Santa Biblia delante de la congregación.
I went to pray in the cathedral.
Fui a rezar a la catedral.
Merry Christmas and Happy New Year to all my friends and family.
Feliz Navidad y feliz año nuevo a todos mis amigos y familiares.
Peter is a famous saint in Christianity.
Peter es un santo famoso en el cristianismo.
The priest baptized the baby in the blessed holy water.
El sacerdote bautizó al bebé con la agua bendita.
The devil and the demons are from hell.
El diablo y los demonios son del infierno.
Many schools refuse to teach evolution.
Muchas escuelas se niegan a enseñar la evolución.

Religion & Holidays

Jew - Judío / **(f)** Judía
Judaism - Judaísmo
Hanukkah - Januca
Menorah - Candelabra de nueve velas
Dreidle - Trompo
Passover - Pascua
Kosher - Casher
Circumcision - Circuncisión
Synagogue - Sinagoga
Goblet - Copa / **Wine -** Vino
Religious - Religioso / **(f)** religiosa
Monotheism - Monoteísmo
Islam - Islam / **Muslim -** Musulmán / **Mohammed -** Mohamed / **Mosque -** Mezquita
Hindu - Hindú / **Buddhist -** Budista / **Temple -** Templo

The Jews worship at the synagogue.
Los judíos rezan en la sinagoga.
The Bible is a holy book which tells the story of the Jewish nations and includes many miracles.
La Biblia es un libro sagrado que cuenta la historia de la nacion judía e incluye muchos milagros.
In Judaism, they pray three times a day. Morning prayer, afternoon prayer, and evening prayer.
En el judaísmo, rezan tres veces al día. Oración de la mañana, oración de la tarde y oración de la noche.
Where is the goblet of wine for Rosh Hashana?
¿Dónde está la copa de vino para Rosh Hashana / el año nuevo de los judios?
The three forefathers are Abraham, Isaac, and Jacob.
Los tres padres antepasados son Abraham, Isaac y Jacob.
I have a menorah and a dreidel for Chanukah.
Tengo una menorá y un trompo para Januca.
Passover is my favorite holiday.
Las pascuas son mi fiesta favorita.
We welcome the Sabbath by lighting candles.
Damos la bienvenida al sábado encendiendo velas.
I want to keep kosher.
Quiero mantenerme casher.
To learn about the Holocaust and the concentration camps is very important.
Aprender sobre el Holocausto y los campos de concentración es muy importante.
Muslims worship at the mosque.
Los musulmanes adoran en la mezquita.
In Islam you must pray five times a day.
En el Islam debes rezar cinco veces al día.

WEDDING AND RELATIONSHIP - BODA Y RELACIÓN

Wedding - Boda
Wedding hall - Salon de bodas
Married - Casado
Civil wedding - Boda civil
Bride - Novia
Groom - Novio
Ceremony - Ceremonia
Reception hall - Pasillo de recepción
Chapel - Capilla
Engagement - Compromiso
Engagement ring - Anillo de compromiso
Wedding ring - Anillo de bodas
Anniversary - Aniversario
Honeymoon - Luna de miel
Fiancé - Prometido / **(f)** prometida
Husband - Marido / esposo
Wife - Mujer/ esposa

They are finally married so now it's time for the honeymoon.
Finalmente están casados, así que ahora es el momento de la luna de miel.
When is the wedding?
¿Cuándo es la boda?
We are having the service in the chapel and the reception in the wedding hall.
Estamos teniendo el servicio en la capilla y la recepción en el salón de bodas.
Our anniversary is on Valentine's Day.
Nuestro aniversario es el día de San Valentín.
This is my engagement ring and this is my wedding ring.
Este es mi anillo de compromiso y este es mi anillo de bodas.
He decided to propose to his girlfriend. She said "yes" and now they are engaged.
Decidió proponerle matrimonio a su novia. Ella dijo "sí" y ahora están comprometidos.
He is my fiancé now. Next year he will be my husband.
Él es mi prometido ahora. El año que viene será mi esposo.
There are three civil weddings at the courthouse today.
Hoy hay tres bodas civiles en el juzgado.
The bride and groom received many presents.
La novia y el novio recibieron muchos regalos.

Valentine day - Día de San Valentín
Love - Amor
In love - Enamorado
To love - Amar
Romantic - Romántico
Darling - Cariño
A date - Una cita
Relationship - Relación
Boyfriend - Novio
Girlfriend - Novia
To hug - Abrazar
A hug - Un abrazo
To kiss - Besar
A kiss - Un beso
Single - Soltero / **(f)** soltera
Divorced - Divorciado / **(f)** divorciada
Widow - Viudo / **(f)** viuda

I am in love with him.
Estoy enamorada de el.
You are very romantic.
Eres muy romantico.
They have a very good relationship.
Tienen una muy buena relación.
I am single because I divorced my wife.
Soy soltero porque me divorcié de mi esposa.
She is my darling and my love.
Ella es mi enamorada y mi amor.
I want to kiss you and hug you in this picture.
Quiero besarte y abrazarte en esta foto.

POLITICS - POLÍTICA

Politics - Política
Flag - Bandera
National anthem - Himno Nacional
Nation - Nación
National - Nacional
International - Internacional
Local - Local
Patriot - Patriota
Symbol - Símbolo
Peace - Paz
Treaty - Trato
State - Estado
County - Condado
Country - País
Century - Siglo
Annexation - Anexión
Plan - Plan
Strategic - Estratégica
Decision - Decisión

This is a political movement which has the support of the majority.
Este es un movimiento político que cuenta con el apoyo de la mayoría.
This flag is the national symbol of the country.
Esta bandera es el símbolo nacional del país.
This is all politics.
Esto es todo política.
There is a difference between state law and local law.
Hay una diferencia entre la ley estatal y la ley local.
He is a patriot of the nation.
Es un patriota de la nación.
Most countries have a national anthem.
La mayoría de los países tienen un himno nacional.
This is a political campaign to demand independence.
Esta es una campaña política para exigir independencia.
The annexation plan was a strategic decision.
El plan de anexión fue una decisión estratégica.

Legal - Legal
Law - Ley
Illegal - Ilegal
International law - Ley internacional
Human rights - Derechos humanos
Punishment - Castigo
Torture - Tortura
Execution - Ejecución
Spy - Espía
Amnesty - Amnistía
Political asylum - Asilo político
Republic - República
Dictator - Dictador
Citizen - Ciudadano
Resident - Residente
Immigrant - Inmigrante
Public - Público
Private - Privado
Racism - Racismo
Government - Gobierno
Revolution - Revolución
Civilian - Civil
Population - Población
Socialism - Socialismo
Communism - Comunismo

In which county is this legal?
¿En qué condado es esto legal?
There were many protests and riots today.
Hubieron muchas protestas y disturbios hoy.
The civilian population wanted a revolution.
La población civil quería una revolución.
The politicians want to ask the president to give the captured spy amnesty.
Los políticos quieren pedirle al presidente que otorgue al espía capturado la amnistía.
Although he was the brutal dictator of the republic, in private he was a nice person.
Aunque era el dictador bruto de la república, en privado era una buena persona.
In some countries torture and execution is a common form of punishment.
En algunos países la tortura y la ejecución son una forma de un castigo común.
This is a violation of human rights and international law.
Esto es una violación de los derechos humanos y el derecho internacional.
Communism and socialism were popular in the 19th century.
El comunismo y el socialismo fuern populares en el siglo dies y nueve.

Politics

President - Presidente
Statement - Declaración
Presidential - Presidencial
Election - Elección
Poll - Encuesta
Campaign - Campaña
Candidate - Candidato
Democracy - Democracia
Movement - Movimiento
Politician - Político
Politics - Política
Campaign - Campaña
To vote - Votar
Majority - Mayoria
Independence - Independencia
Party - Partido
Veto - Veto
Impeachment - El proceso de destitución
Vice president - Vice presidente
Defense Secretary - Secretario de Defensa
Prime minister - Primer ministro
Interior minister - Ministro del Interior
Exterior minister - Ministro del exterior
Convoy - Convoy

They want to appoint him as defense minister.
Quieren nombrarlo como ministro de defensa.
Both parties want to veto the impeachment inquiry.
Ambos partidos quieren vetar la investigación de juicio político.
I want to see the presidential convoy.
Quiero ver el convoy presidencial.
In some countries other than the United States, they have a prime minister, interior minister, and exterior minister.
E n algunos países, fuera de los Estados Unidos, tienen un primer ministro, un ministro del interior y ministro de exteriores.
I want to meet the president and the vice president today.
Quiero reunirme con el presidente y el vicepresidente hoy.
I want to go to the election polls to vote for the new candidate.
Quiero ir a las urnas electorales para votar por el nuevo candidato.
We support democracy and are against fascism and racism.
Apoyamos la democracia y estamos en contra del fascismo y el racismo.

United Nations - Naciones Unidas
Condemnation - Condenación
United States - Estados Unidos
European Union - Unión Europea
Coup - Golpe
Treason - Traición
Fascism - Fascismo
Resistance - Resistencia
Members - Miembros
Captured - Capturado
Ambassador - Embajador
Embassy - Embajada
Consulate - Consulado
Biased - Sesgado
Unilateral - Unilateral
Bilateral - Bilateral
Resolution - Resolución
Rebels - Rebeldes
Sanctions - Sanciones

All the members of the resistance were accused of treason and had to ask for political asylum.
Todos los miembros de la resistencia fueron acusados de traición y tuvieron que pedir asilo político.
The resolution is biased.
La resolución es parcial.
This was an official condemnation.
Esta fue una condena oficial.
The United Nations is located in New York.
Las oficinas de las Naciones Unidas se encuentran en Nueva York.
I am a United States citizen and a resident of the European Union.
Soy ciudadano de los Estados Unidos y residente de la Unión Europea.
The ambassador's residence is located near the embassy.
La residencia del embajador se encuentra cerca de la embajada.
I need the phone number and address of the consulate.
Necesito el número de teléfono y la dirección del consulado.
Are consular services available today?
¿Hay servicios consulares disponibles hoy?
The international peace treaty needs to include both sides.
El tratado de paz internacional debe incluir a ambas partes.
According to the government, the rebels carried out an illegal coup.
Según el gobierno, los rebeldes llevaron a cabo un golpe ilegal.
They must impose sanctions against that country.
Deben imponer sanciones contra ese país.

MILITARY - MILITAR

Army - Ejército / **Armed forces -** Fuerzas armadas
Navy - Marina de guerra
Soldier - Soldado / **Troops -** Tropas
A force - Una fuerza / **Ground forces -** Tropas terrestres
Base - Base / **Headquarter -** Cuartel general / **Intelligence -** Inteligencia
Ranks - Rangos / **Sergeant -** Sargento / **Lieutenant -** Teniente
The general - El general / **Commander -** Comandante / **Captain -** Capitán
Chief of Staff - Jefe de estado mayor
Enlistment - Alistamiento
Reserves - Reservas
War - Guerra
Terrorism - Terrorismo / **Terrorist -** Terrorista / **Insurgency -** Insurrección
Border crossing - Cruce de las fronteras
Refugee - Refugiado
Camp - Campo

I want to enlist in the military.
Quiero enlistrarme en el ejército.
This is a base for military aircrafts only.
Esta es una base solo para aviones militares.
That is the headquarters of the enemy.
Esa es la sede del enemigo.
The Air Force is a branch of the military.
La Fuerza Aérea es una rama de las fuerzas armadas.
They need to enlist reserve forces for the war.
Necesitan reclutar fuerzas de reserva para la guerra.
Welcome to the border crossing.
Bienvenido al cruce de las fronteras.
Military intelligence relies on important sources of information to provide direction and guidance.
La inteligencia militar se basa en importantes fuentes de información para proporcionar dirección y orientación.
The chief of staff was the target of a failed assassination attempt.
El jefe de gabinete fue blanco de un intento fallido de asesinato.
The sniper killed the highest-ranking lieutenant.
El francotirador mató al teniente de más alto rango.
The terrorist group claimed responsibility for the car-bomb attack at the refugee camp.
El grupo terrorista se atribuyó la responsabilidad del ataque con coche bomba en el campo de refugiados.
It's impossible to defeat terrorism because it's an ideology.
Es imposible vencer al terrorismo porque es una ideología.

Air strike - Ataque aéreo
Air force - Fuerza Aerea / **Fighter jet -** Avión de combate
Military aircraft - Aeronave militar
Drone - Zumbido / **Stealth technology -** Tecnología sigilosa
Tank - Tanque
Submarine - Submarino
Weapon - Arma
Grenade - Granada / **Mine -** Mía / **Bomb -** Bomba
Sniper - Francotirador / **Gun -** Pistola / **Rifle -** Escopeta, rifle / **Bullet -** Bala
Missile - Misil / **Mortar -** Mortero
Anti tank missile - Misil antitanque / **Anti aircraft missile -** Misil antiaéreo
Shoulder fire missile - Misil de fuego de hombro
Ammunition - Munición / **Artillery -** Artillería / **Artillery shell -** Proyectil de artillería
Ballistic missile - Misil balístico
Atomic bomb - Bomba atómica
Weapon of mass destruction - Arma de destrucción masiva
Chemical weapon - Arma química
Explosion - Explosión
Flare system - Sistema de antorchas
Supply - Suministro / **Storage -** Almacenamiento
Armor - Armadura

The M-16 is a US-made rifle.
El M-16 es un rifle de fabricación estadounidense.
The tank fired artillery shells.
El tanque disparó proyectiles de artillería.
Shoulder-fired missiles are extremely dangerous and are hard to defend against.
Los misiles de hombro son extremadamente peligrosos y son difíciles de defenderse.
The flare system is meant as a defense against anti-aircraft missiles.
El sistema de bengalas pretende ser una defensa contra misiles antiaéreos.
The navy is able to intercept missiles.
La marina puede interceptar misiles.
At the terrorist safe-house, guns, bullets, and grenades were found.
En el refugio de terroristas, se encontraron pistolas, balas y granadas.
The coalition forces struck an enemy arms depot.
Las fuerzas de la coalición atacaron un depósito de armas del enemigo.
An intense missile attack was carried out against the supply forces that resulted in many casualties.
Se llevó a cabo un intenso ataque con misiles contra las fuerzas de suministro que resultó en muchas víctimas.
The terrorist group fired ballistic missiles at the nuclear facility site.
El grupo terrorista disparó misiles balísticos contra el sitio de la instalación nuclear.
Atomic bombs and chemical weapons are weapons of mass destruction.
Las bombas atómicas y las armas químicas son armas de destrucción masiva.

Military

A target - On objetivo / **To target -** Apuntar
An attack - Un ataque / **To attack -** Atacar / **Intense -** Intenso
To shoot - Disparar / **Open fire -** Abran fuego / **Fired -** Despedido
Assassination - Asesinato / **Assassin -** Asesino
Enemy - Enemigo
Reconnaissance - Reconocimiento / **To infiltrate -** Infiltrarse / **Invasion -** Invasión
Exchange of fire - Intercambio de fuego
A cease fire - Un alto el fuego / **Withdrawal -** Retiro
To defeat - Derrotar
To surrender - Rendirse
Victim - Víctima / **Injury -** Lesión / **Wounded -** Herido
Deaths - Muertes / **Killed -** Matado / **To kill -** Matar
Prisoner of war - Prisionero de guerra / **Missing in action -** Perdido en acción
Act of war - Acto de guerra
War crimes - Crímenes de guerra
Defense - Defensa
Attempt - Intento

There is an invasion of ground forces.
Hay una invasión de las fuerzas terrestres.
The soldier wanted to open fire and shoot at the invading forces.
El soldado quería abrir fuego y disparó a las fuerzas invasoras.
The bomb attack was considered an act of aggression and an act of war.
El ataque con bomba fue considerado un acto de agresión y un acto de guerra.
The reconnaissance drone managed to infiltrate deep within enemy territory.
El avión no tripulado de reconocimiento logró infiltrarse en las profundidades del territorio enemigo.
The airstrike targeted an ammunition storage site.
El ataque aéreo apuntó a un sitio de almacenamiento de municiones.
The mortar attack and exchange of fire caused injuries and deaths on both sides.
El ataque con mortero y el intercambio de fuego causaron heridas y muerte en ambos lados.
First, we need to clear the mines.
Primero, necesitamos eliminar las minas.
The ceasefire agreement included the release of prisoners of war.
El acuerdo de alto de fuego incluyó la liberación de prisioneros de guerra.
The army made a public statement to announce the withdrawal.
El ejército hizo una declaración pública para anunciar la retirada.
There was a huge explosion as a result of the terrorist attack.
Hubo una gran explosión como resultado del ataque terrorista.
The commander of the insurgency was accused of serious war crimes.
El comandante de la insurgencia fue acusado de graves crímenes de guerra.
Several of the submarine sailors were missing in action.
Varios marineros submarinos desaparecieron en acción.

Basic Grammatical Requirements of the Spanish Language

Present Tense Indicative: Regular Verbs

In the Spanish language all infinitive forms of the verbs end in: "ar", "er", "ir".
The verbs are conjugated in the present tense of the indicative form by just adding the following personal endings to the stem of the verb.

	Hablar	Comer	Vivir
Yo	hablo	como	vivo
Tu	hablas	comes	vives
El, ella, usted	habla	come	vive
Nostro/as	hablamos	comemos	vivemos
Vosotros/as	hablais	comeis	vivis
Ellos, ellas, ustedes	hablan	comen	viven

AR VERBS   **ER VERBS**   **IR VERBS**

The asterick represents irregular verbs.

AR VERBS	ER VERBS	IR VERBS
Comprar - To buy	**Beber** - To drink	**Abrir** - To open
Bailar - To dance	**Comer** - To eat	**Escribir** - To write
Cambiar - To change	**Leer** - To read	**Assistir** - To assist
Desear - To wish	**Creer** - To believe	**Insistir** - To insist
Preguntar - To ask	**Responder** - To respond	**Recibir** - To receive
Trabajar - To work	**Vender** - To sell	*****Preferir** - To prefer
Necesitar - To need	**Leer** - To read	*****Incluir** - To include
Tomar - To take	*****Querer** - To want	*****Salir** - To leave
Llegar - To arrive	**Obedecer** - To obey	*****Servir** - To serve
Ayudar - To help	*****Tener** - To have	*****Decir** - To say
Estudiar - To study	**Comprender** - To understand	*****Sentir** - To feel
Escuchar - To hear	*****Saber** - To know	
Viajar - To travel		
Demorar - To delay		
Terminar - To finish		
Pagar - To pay		

The Articles "the" and "a"

In Spanish, nouns are plural or singular as well as masculine or feminine. For example, the article "the" for Spanish, nouns ending with an *a*, *e*, and *i* (usually deemed as feminine) is typically *la*. For nouns ending with an *o*, or a consonant, then the noun is generally masculine, and the article is usually *el*. In plural form is *los* for masculine forms and *las* for feminine forms. "The boy" is *el* (the) *niño* (boy), "the girl" is *la niña*, "the boys" are *los niños*, and "the girls" are *las niñas*. ("the house" is *la casa*, "the car" is *el auto*). Although there are exceptions, such as for words that end with *ma*, *pa*, and *ta*, the article is usually *el*. Plus, some nouns are considered irregular and must be memorized. For example, "the problem" is *el problema* and not *la problema*. Also, the "wall" *la pared* or "the water" *el agua*.

For the article "a" (*un* and *una*), its conjugation is determined by feminine and masculine forms, "a car"—*un auto*, "a house"—*una casa*.

The conjugation for "this" (*esta*, *este*, *estos*, and *estas*) and "that" (*ese*, *esa*, *esos*, *esas*) is similar. "This," *este*, is masculine, for example, *este libro* ("this book"). Feminine is *esta*, for instance, *esta casa* ("this house"). *Estos libros* ("these books") and *estas casas* ("these houses") is the plural form. "That," *ese*, is masculine, that is, *ese libro* (that book). Feminine would be *esa*, for example, *esa silla* ("that chair"). In plural, this is *esos libros* ("those books) and *esas sillas* ("those chairs").

Temporary and Permanent

The different forms of "is" are *es* and *esta*. When referring to a permanent condition, for example, "she is a girl" (*ella es una niña*), you use *es*. For temporary positions, "the girl is doing well today" (*la chica esta muy bien hoy*), you use *esta*. However, *está* is also used to indicate a permanent location, for example, "Spain is located in Europe" / *España está ubicada en Europa*.

"You are" or "are you" could be translated as *estas*, or they could also be translated as *tú eres*. An example of temporary position is "how are you today?" (*cómo estas hoy*). And another example of temporary position is "you are here" (*estas aqui*). Another example of permanent position is "are you Mexican?" (*tú eres Mexicano?*) as well as "you are a man!" (tú eres un hombre!). Both derive from the verbs *ser* (permanent) and *estar* (temporary).

* **"I am"—*estoy* and *yo soy*.** *Yo soy* refers to a permanent condition: "I am Italian" / *Yo soy Italiano*. Temporary condition would be "I am at the mall" / *Estoy en el mall*.

* **"We are"—*somos* (permanent) and *estamos* (temporary).** *Somos Peruvianos* / "we are Peruvian" and *estamos en el parque* / "we are at the park."

* **"They are"—*son* (permanent)** *ellos son Chilenos* / "they are Chileans", **and *estan* (temporary)** *ellos estan en el auto* / "they are in the car."

Basic Grammatical Requirements of the Spanish Language

Eso and *esto* are neuter pronouns, meaning they don't have a gender. They usually refer to an idea or an unknown object that isn't specifically named, for example, "that"/ *eso*; "that is"/ *eso es*; "because of that" / *por eso*; "this" / *esto*; "this is good" / *esto es bien;* and "what is this?" / *qué es esto?*

In regards to "my," singular and plural form exists as well, *mi* and *mis*.

* "my chair" / *mi silla*
* "my chairs" / *mis sillas*

With regard to "your," *tu* and *tus*, the singular is *tu*, as in *tu auto* / "your car," and the plural is *tus* (e.g., *tus autos* / your cars).

Verb Conjugation

The word "I" (*yo*) before a conjugated verb isn't required. For example, *yo necesito saber la fecha* ("I need to know the date") can be said, *Necesito saber la fecha* because *necesito* already means "I need" in conjugated form, although saying *yo* isn't incorrect! The same can also be said with *tú / te, el / ella, nosotros, ellos / ellas,* in which they aren't required to be placed prior to the conjugated verb, but if they are, then it isn't wrong.

Synonyms and Antonyms

There are three ways of describing time.
Vez/veces — "first time" / *primera vez* or "three times" / *tres veces*
Tiempo — "during the time of the dinosaurs" / *durante el tiempo de los dinosaurios*
Hora — "What time is it?" / *Qué hora es?*

Que has four definitions.
"What"—*Que es esto?* / "What is this?"
"Than"—*Estoy mejor que tu* / "I am better than you"
"That"—"I want to say that I am near the house" / *yo quiero decir que estoy acerca de la casa*
"I must" / "I have to"—*Tengo que*. The verb *tener*, "to have," whether it's in conjugated or infinite form, if it is followed by an infinitive verb, then *que* must always follow.

For example:

"I have to swim now" / *tengo que nadar ahora*.

There are two ways of describing "so."
"So"—*entonces*. "So I need to know" / *entonces necesito saber*.
"So"—*tan*. *Eso es tan distante* / "this is so far"

Si and *Sí*
Si (without accent) means "if"
Sí (with accent) means "yes"

Tú, Te, Ti and Tu

There are three different forms of how to use the pronoun "you"—*tú, te,* and *ti.*

Tú is a subject pronoun (second person of singular), referring to the individual who is doing the action. Unlike in English, it isn't required in Spanish. For example, in "you are here" / *estas aquí,* you aren't required to say *tú estas aquí.*

Te is a direct and indirect object pronoun, the person who is actually affected by the action that is being carried out. But the *te* comes before the verb, for example, "I send you" / *Yo te mando* or "I permit you" / *Yo te permito.* In the event the verb is infinitive, then *te* precedes the verb. For example, in the sentence "I want to follow you" / *quiero seguirte, seguir* and the *te* will connect with the verb and become one word.

Ti is a preposition pronoun, meaning it goes with a preposition (like *para, de, por*), for example, *para ti* / "for you" or *yo voy a ti* / "I am going to you" (added *a ti*).

Tu without the accent (´) means "your": *tu casa* / "your house."

Tuyo means "yours" and *tuyos* is plural, for example, *el libro es tuyo* / "the book is yours" and "the books are yours" / *los libros son tuyos.*

Ir a + infinitive and yo voy & me voy

In Spanish "to," *a* (pronounced as "ha"), isn't required between the conjugated verb and the infinitive form. For example, *Yo puedo decir* ("I can say"). But in regards to the verb "to go", *ir,* then the preposition *a* must always follow the *ir,* (whether in the conjugated or infinitive form) before connecting with the infinitive verb. For example, *Yo voy a ver* ("I am going to see") or *Yo necesito ir a buscar* ("I need to go to search"). "I go" and "I am going" could either be translated as *yo voy* or *me voy. Yo voy* refers to going to a specific place, for example, *yo voy a la tienda* ("I am going to the store"). *Me voy* is going somewhere and not specifying the exact destination, for example, *me voy afuera* ("I am going outside").

Using De

De is one of the most crucial prepositions in the Spanish language. Its most common use is much like the English words "from" and "of," but you will encounter it in other situations as well. It could also mean "than," "in," "with," and "by."

Use *de* when referring to "of" and "from."
* "I am from the United States" / *soy de los Estados Unidos.*
* "three more days of summer" / *tres más días de verano.*

Another form of *de* is to indicate the possessor.
* *la casa de Moises* / "Moises's house" or "the house of Moises"
* *las playas de Florida* / "Florida's beaches" or "the beaches of Florida"

Another use for *de* is for preposition phrases.
* *afuera de la casa de tu novia* / "outside the house of your girlfriend"

Basic Grammatical Requirements of the Spanish Language

* *a lado de tu novio* / "next to your boyfriend"
* *alrededor de la picina* / "around the pool"

However, if *de* is followed by *el* then both words combine to form *del*. For example, "from the car" / *del auto,* and **not** *de el auto.*

This should cover the most typical uses of *de*. However, there are other uses which haven't been mentioned here.

Using Lo and La

Lo and *La* are used as direct masculine, feminine, and neuter object pronouns, meaning "him," "her," or "it."

In case the verb is conjugated, *lo* and *la* precede the conjugated verb.

* "I don't want him to know" / *no lo quiero conocer*
* "I don't need her" / *No la necesito*

If the verb is in the infinitive form, then the *lo* and the *la* precede the infinitive verb and connect, creating one word:

* "I want to buy it." / *Quiero comprarlo.*
* "I want to find it." / *Quiero encontrarlo.*
* "I want to see her." / *Quiero verla.*
* "I don't want to know him." / *No quiero conocerlo.*
* "I don't want to give her." / *No quiero darla.*

Another example of using *lo* in Spanish, is, as the abstract neuter article "the".

* "the best of Charlie Chaplin" / *lo mejor de Charlie Chaplin* (since "best" is the abstract neuter noun).

Reflexive Form

In the Spanish language we use *me, te,* and *se* in relation to the reflexive form of a verb, which will be preceding or proceeding that verb, and set as a prefix or suffix. For example, the verb "to wash" - *lavar.*

"I wash myself" - *me lavo,*
"you wash yourself" - *te lavas,*
"he washed himself" - *se lava.*

In the infinitive form it connects as a suffix:
"I want to wash myself" - *quiero lavarme,*
"you wash yourself" - *quieres lavarte,*
"he washed himself" - *quiere lavarse.*

Conclusion

Hopefully, you have enjoyed this book and will use the knowledge you have learned in various situations in your everyday life. In contrast to other methods of learning foreign languages, the theory in this current usage is that ever-greater topics can be broached so that one's vocabulary can expand. This method relies on the discovery I made of the list of core words from each language. Once these are learned, your conversational learning skills will progress very quickly.

You are now ready to discuss sport and school and office-related topics and this will open up your world to a more satisfying extent. Humans are social creatures and language helps us interact. Indeed, at times, it can keep us alive, such as in war situations. You might find yourself in dangerous situations perhaps as a journalist, military personnel or civilian and you need to be armed with the appropriate vocabulary.

"This is a base for military aircraft only," you may have to tell some people who try to enter a field you are protecting, or know what you are being told when someone says to you, "Welcome to the border crossing." As a journalist on a foreign assignment, you may need to quickly understand what you are being told, such as "The sniper killed the highest-ranking lieutenant." If you are someone negotiating on behalf of the army, you may need to find another lieutenant very quickly. Lives, at times, literally depend on your level of understanding and comprehension.

This unique approach that I first discovered when using this method to learn on my own, will have helped you speak the Spanish language much quicker than any other way.

NOTE FROM THE AUTHOR

Thank you for your interest in my work. I encourage you to share your overall experience of this book by posting a review. Your review can make a difference! Please feel free to describe how you benefited from my method or provide creative feedback on how I can improve this program. I am constantly seeking ways to enhance the quality of this product, based on personal testimonials and suggestions from individuals like you. In order to post a review, please check with the retailer of this book.

Thanks and best of luck,

Yatir Nitzany

www.ingramcontent.com/pod-product-compliance
Lightning Source LLC
Chambersburg PA
CBHW050333120526
44592CB00014B/2172